P. ANASTASIA'S

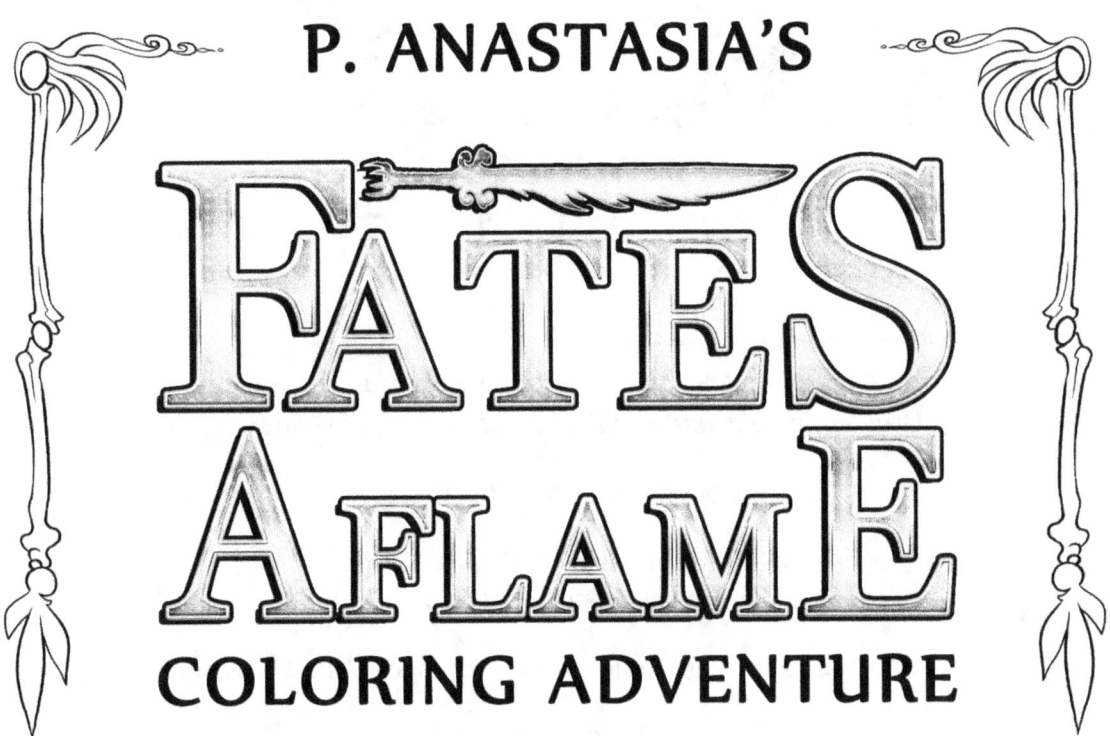

FATES AFLAME
COLORING ADVENTURE

*Unique & Magical Illustrations for **anyone** who likes to color!*

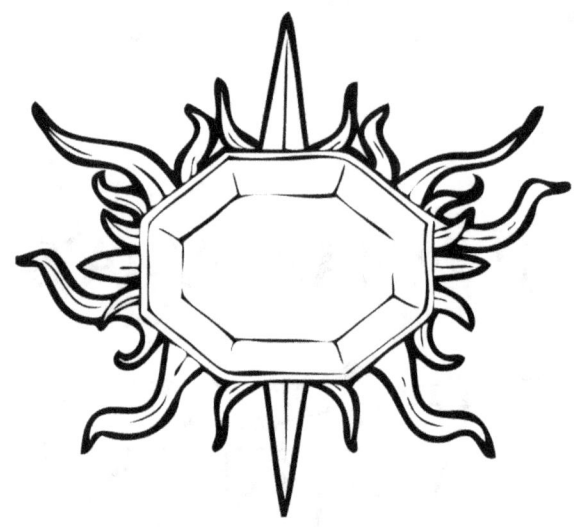

Fates Aflame Coloring Adventure:
Dragons, magic, and mythical creatures from the book series

Copyright © 2017 P. Anastasia

Illustrations by Cristiana Leone
www.CristianaLeone.com

Silver Diamond and Celestial Galaxy logos © P. Anastasia

All rights reserved.

ISBN: 978-0-9974485-2-8

For more information on the Fates Aflame series, visit FatesAflame.com

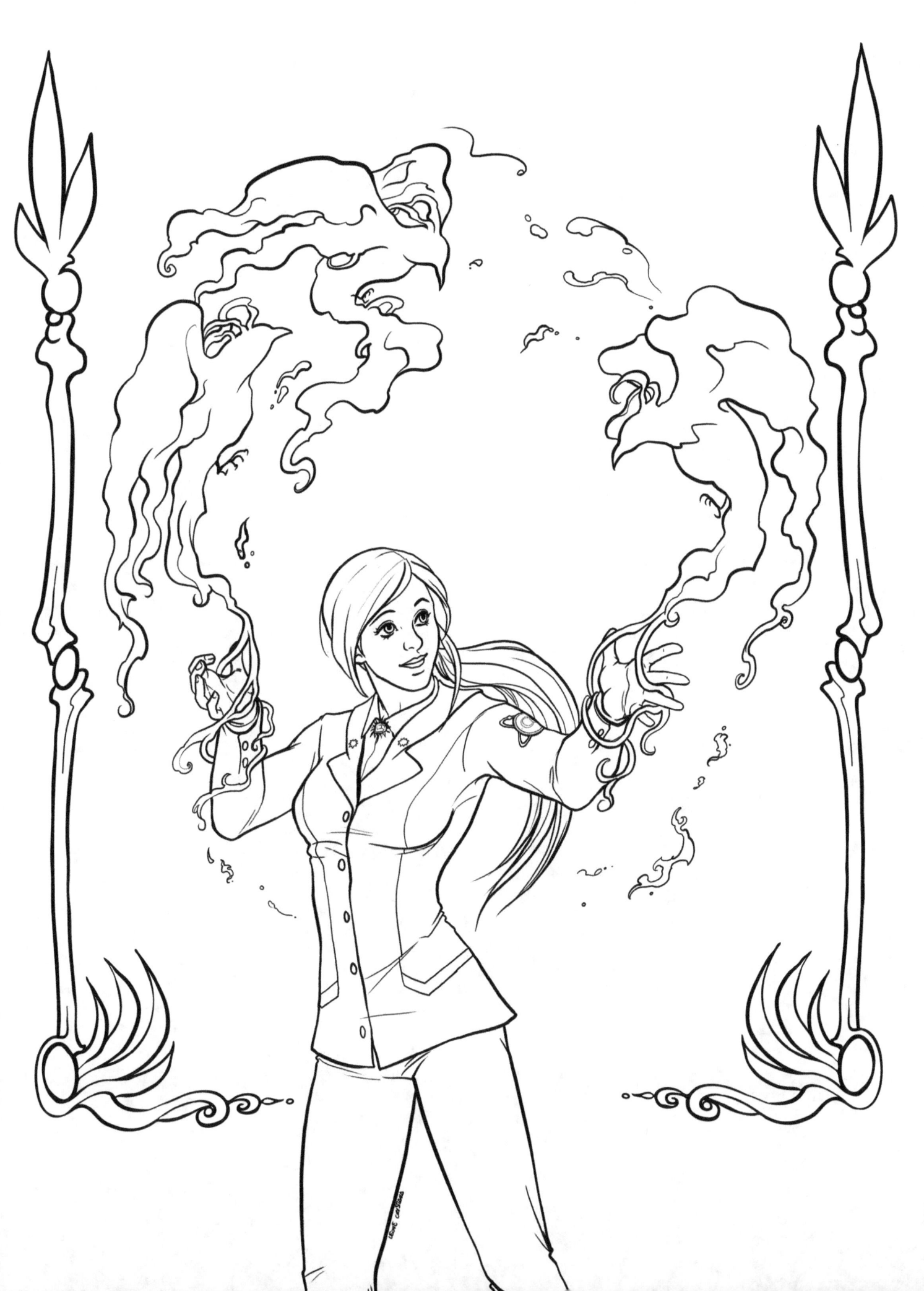

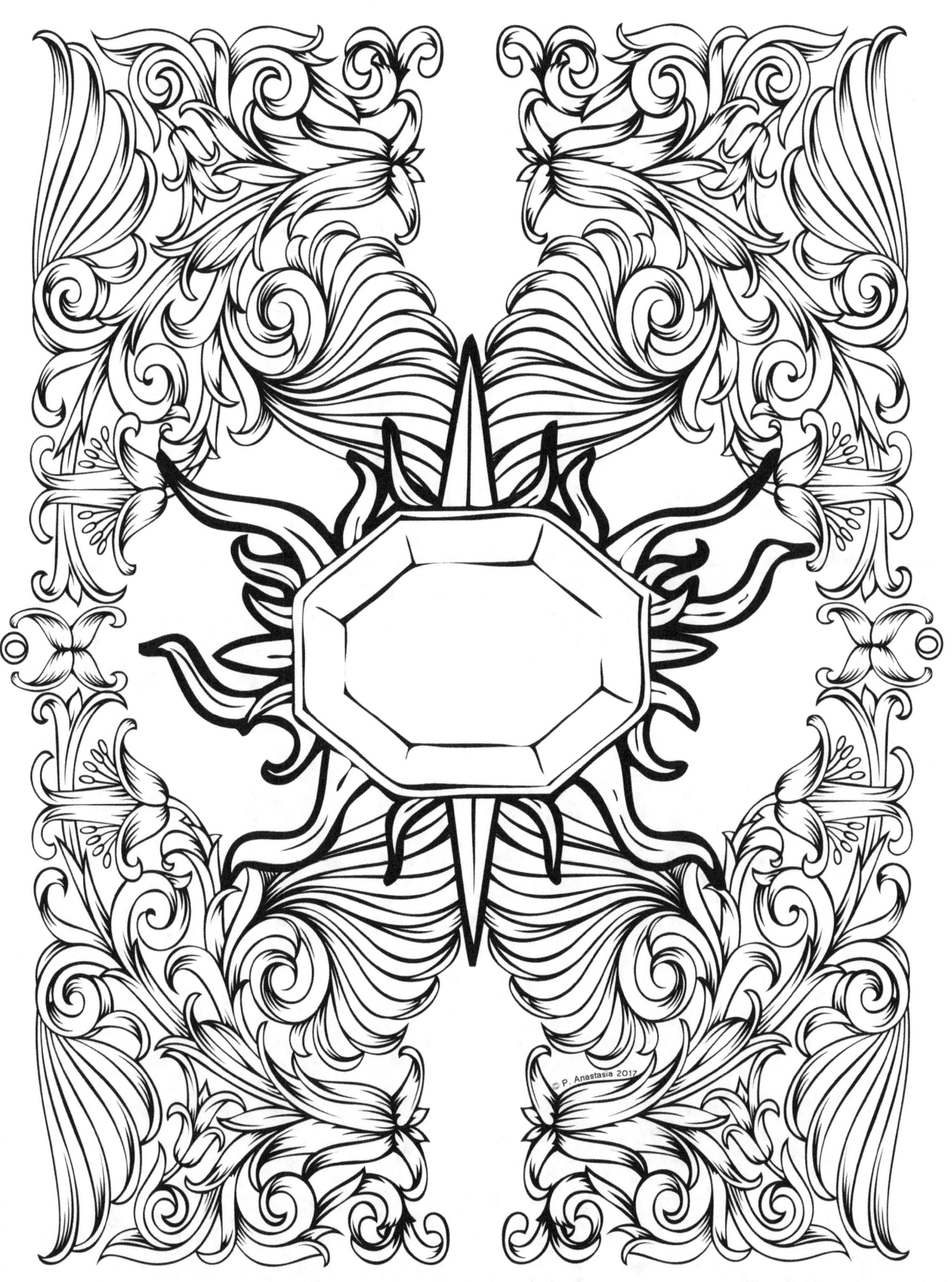

© P. Anastasia 2017

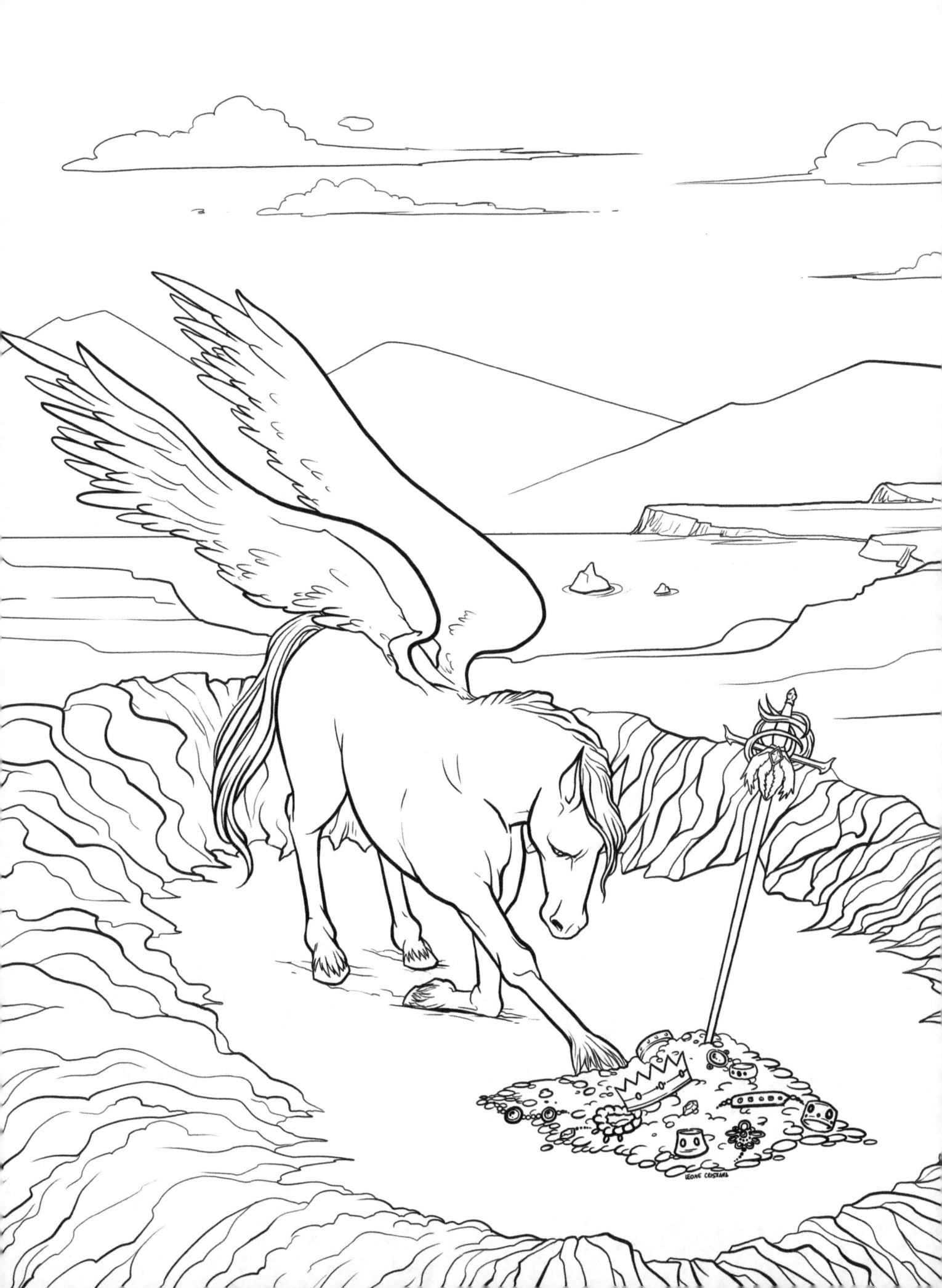

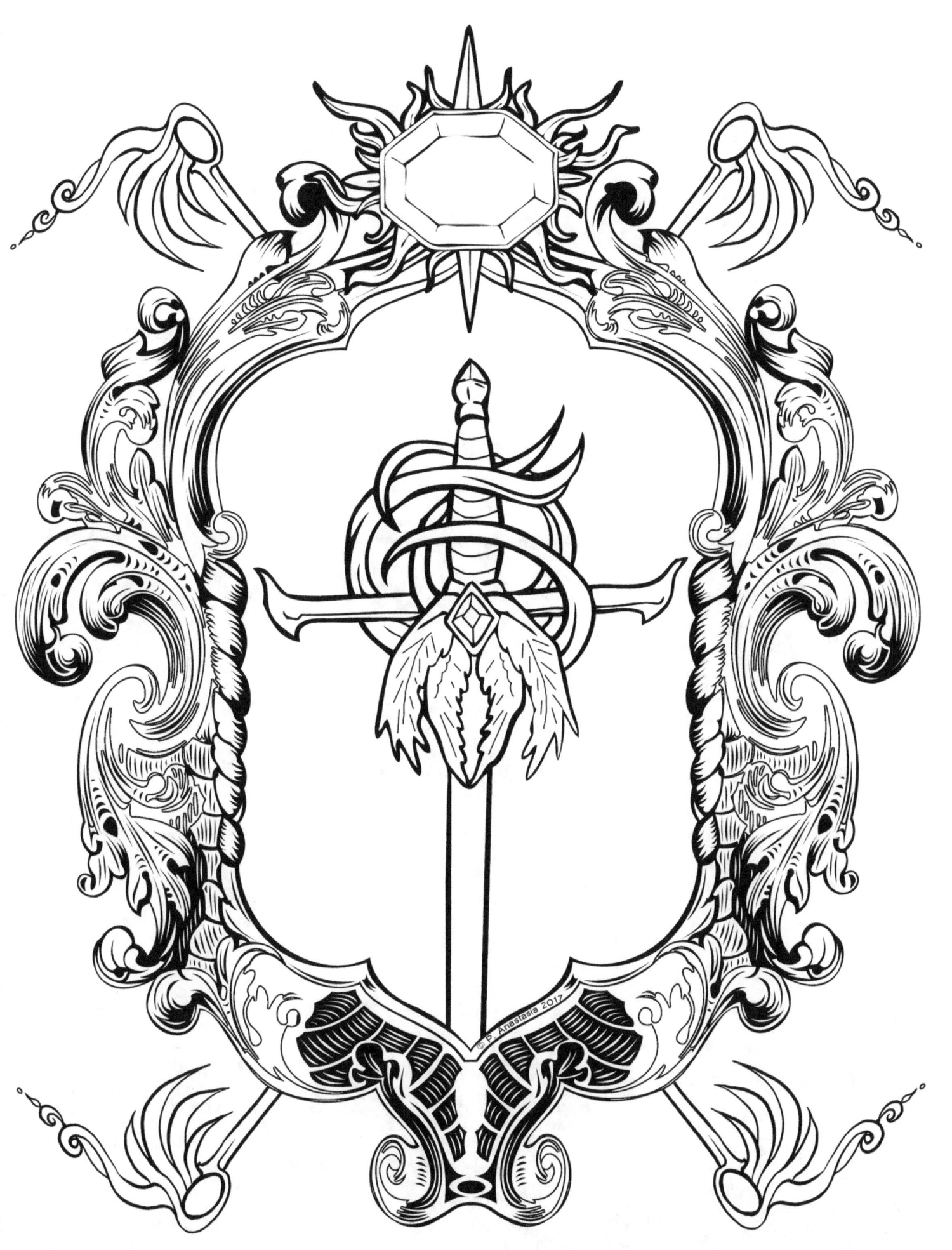

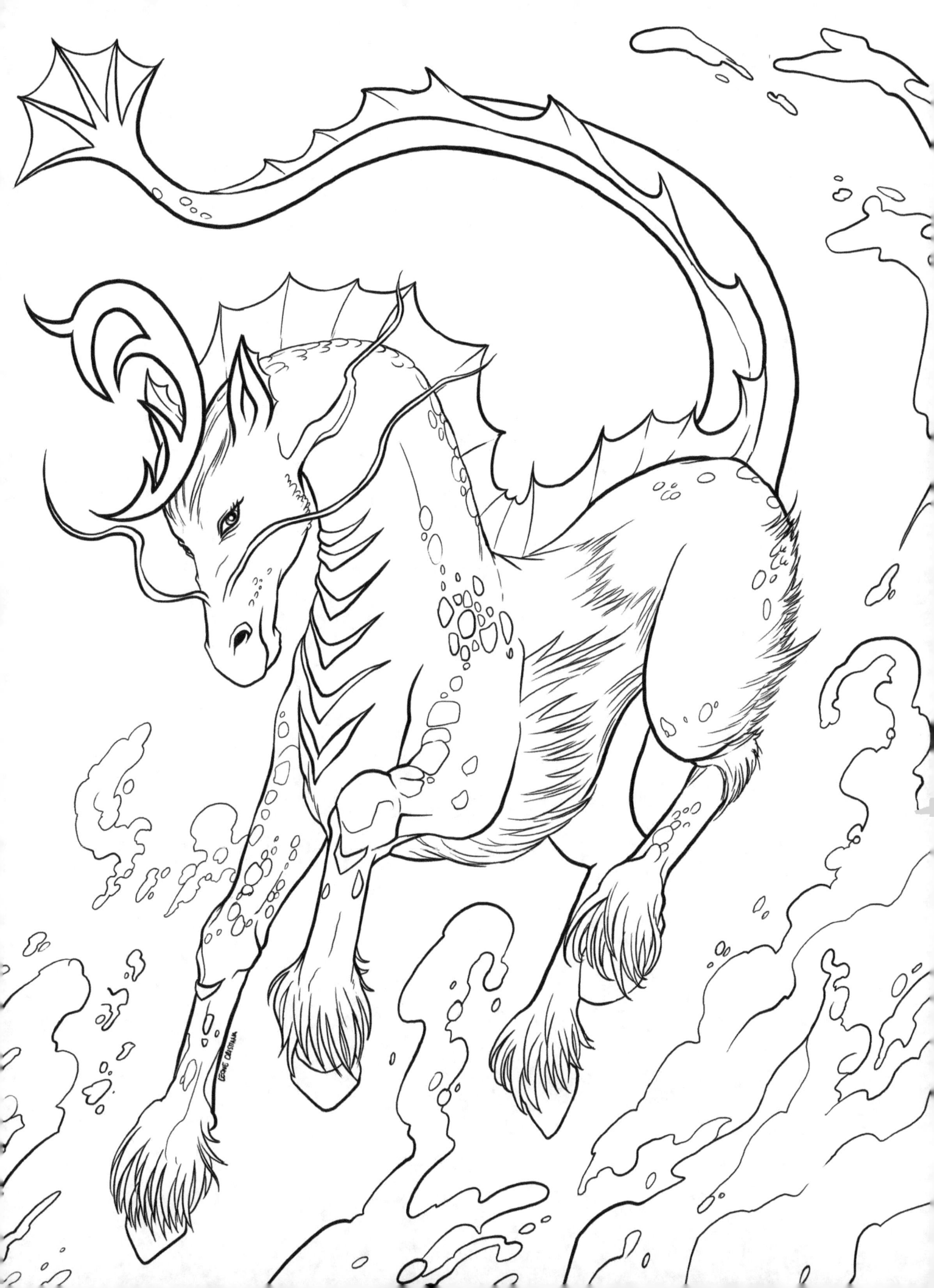

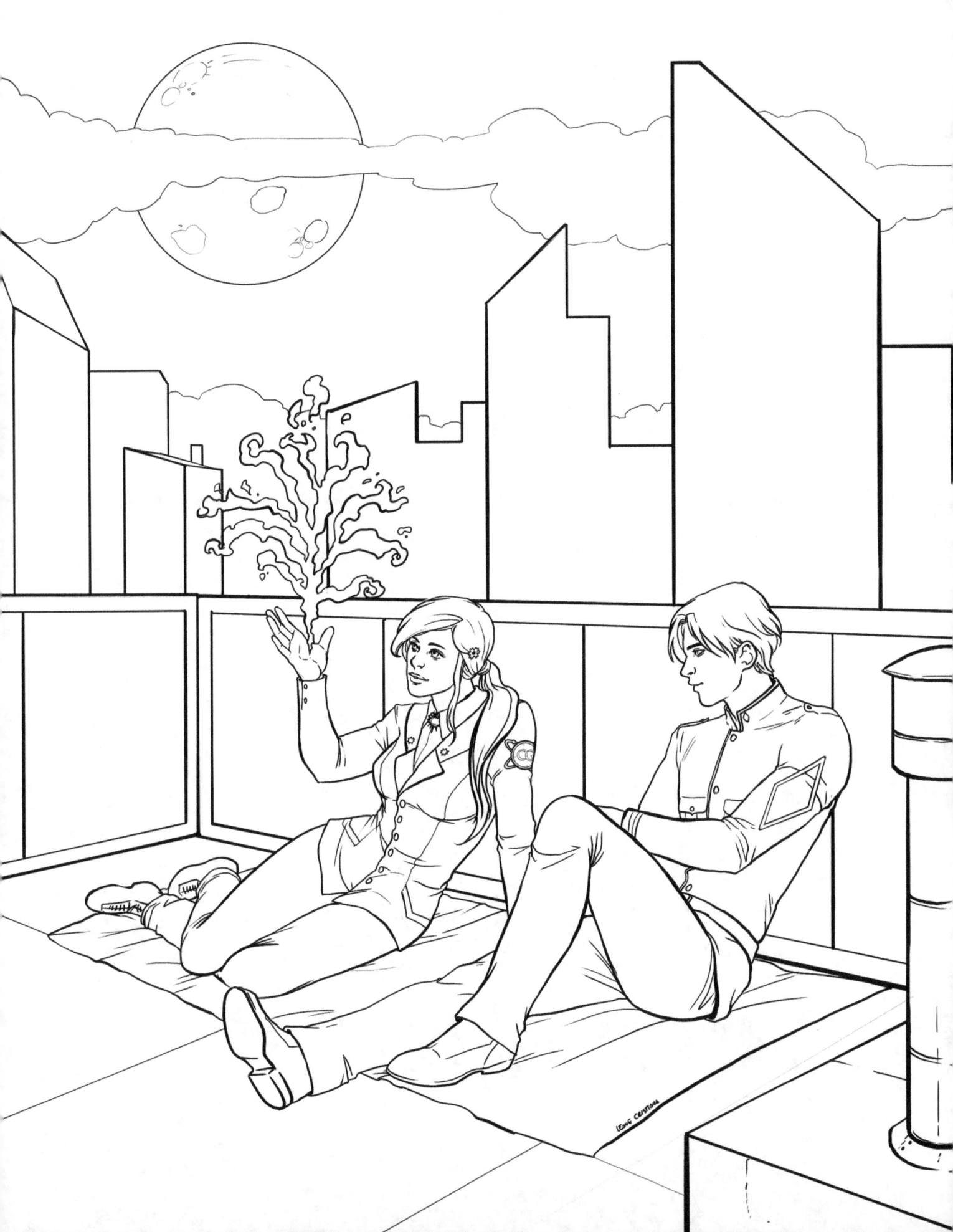

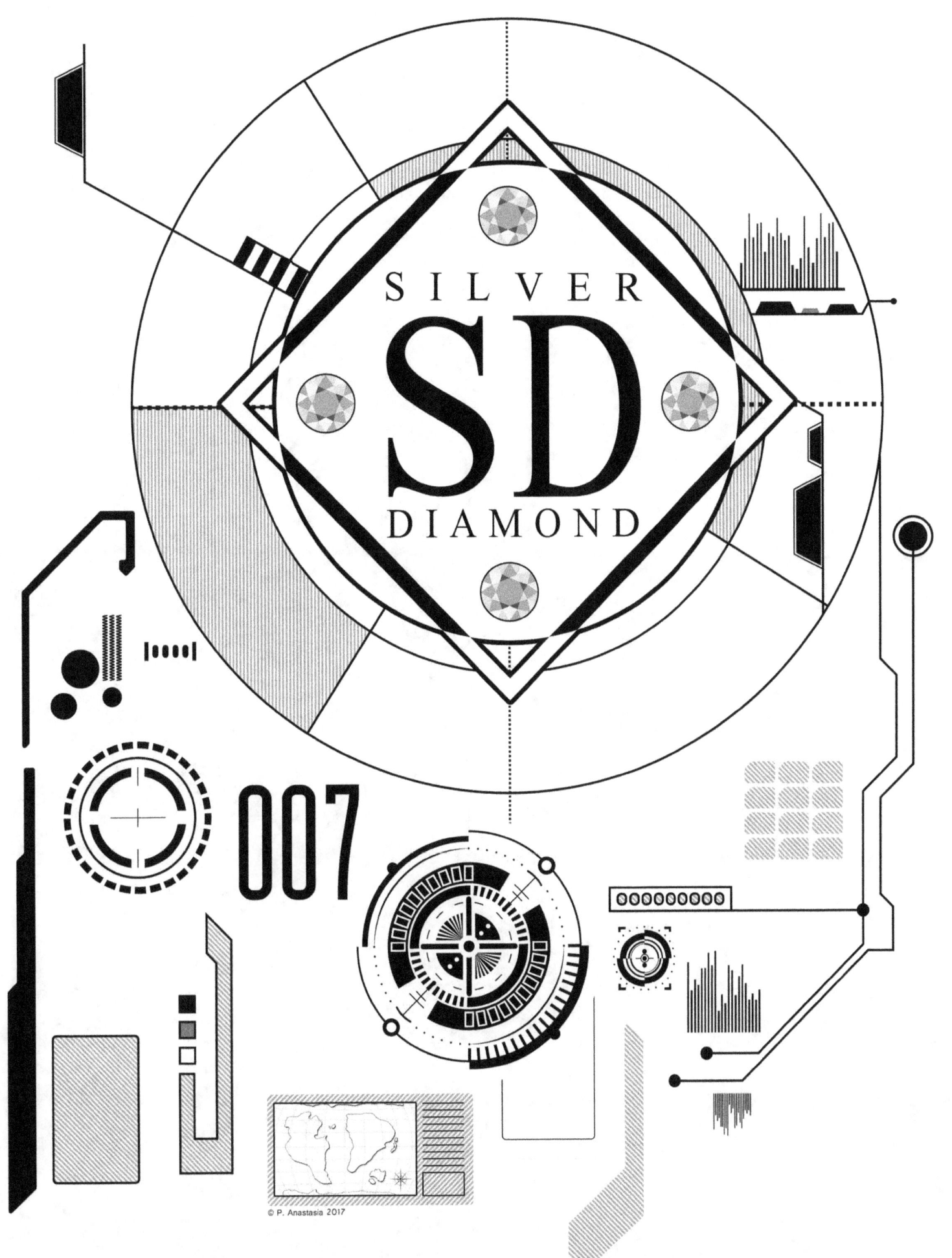

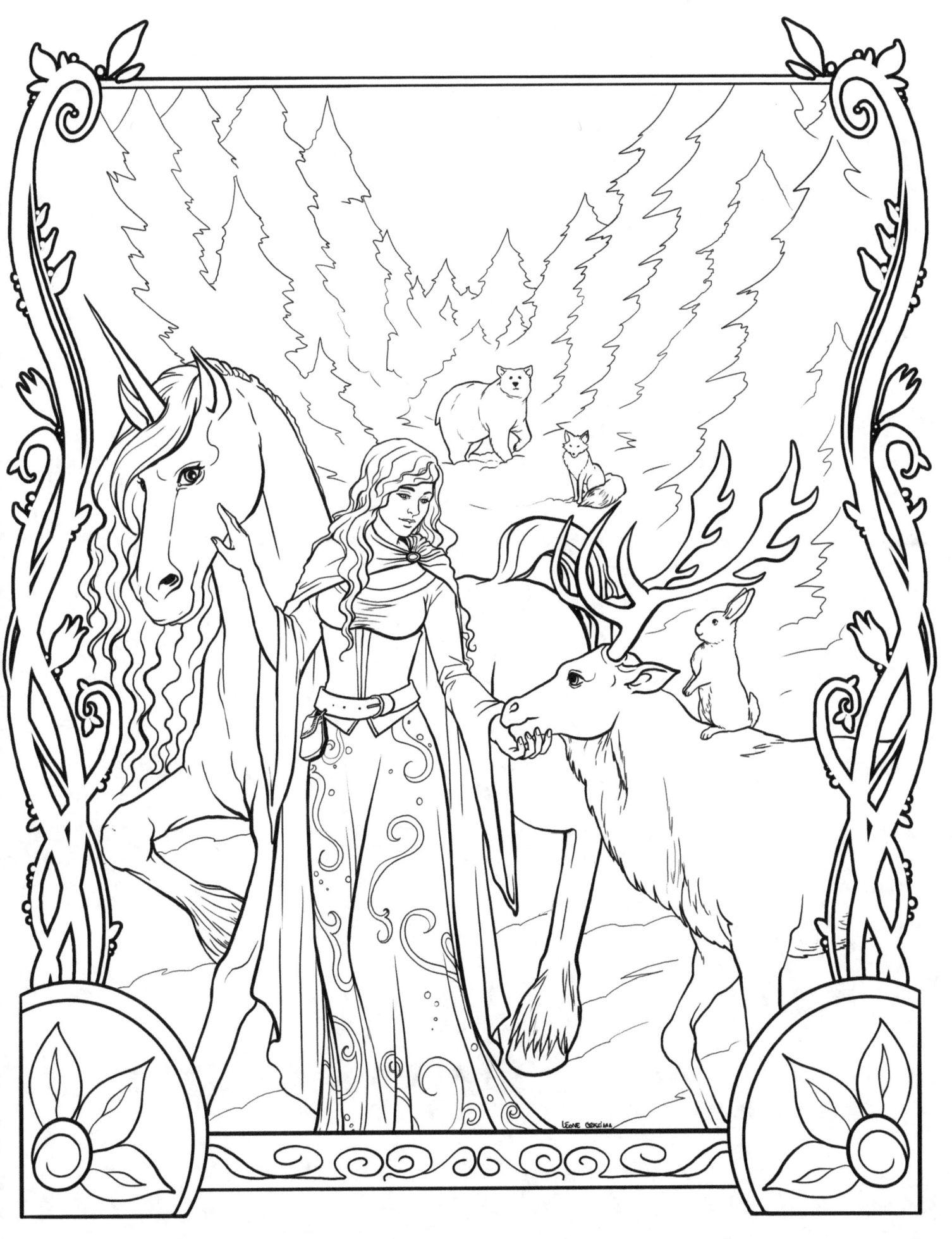

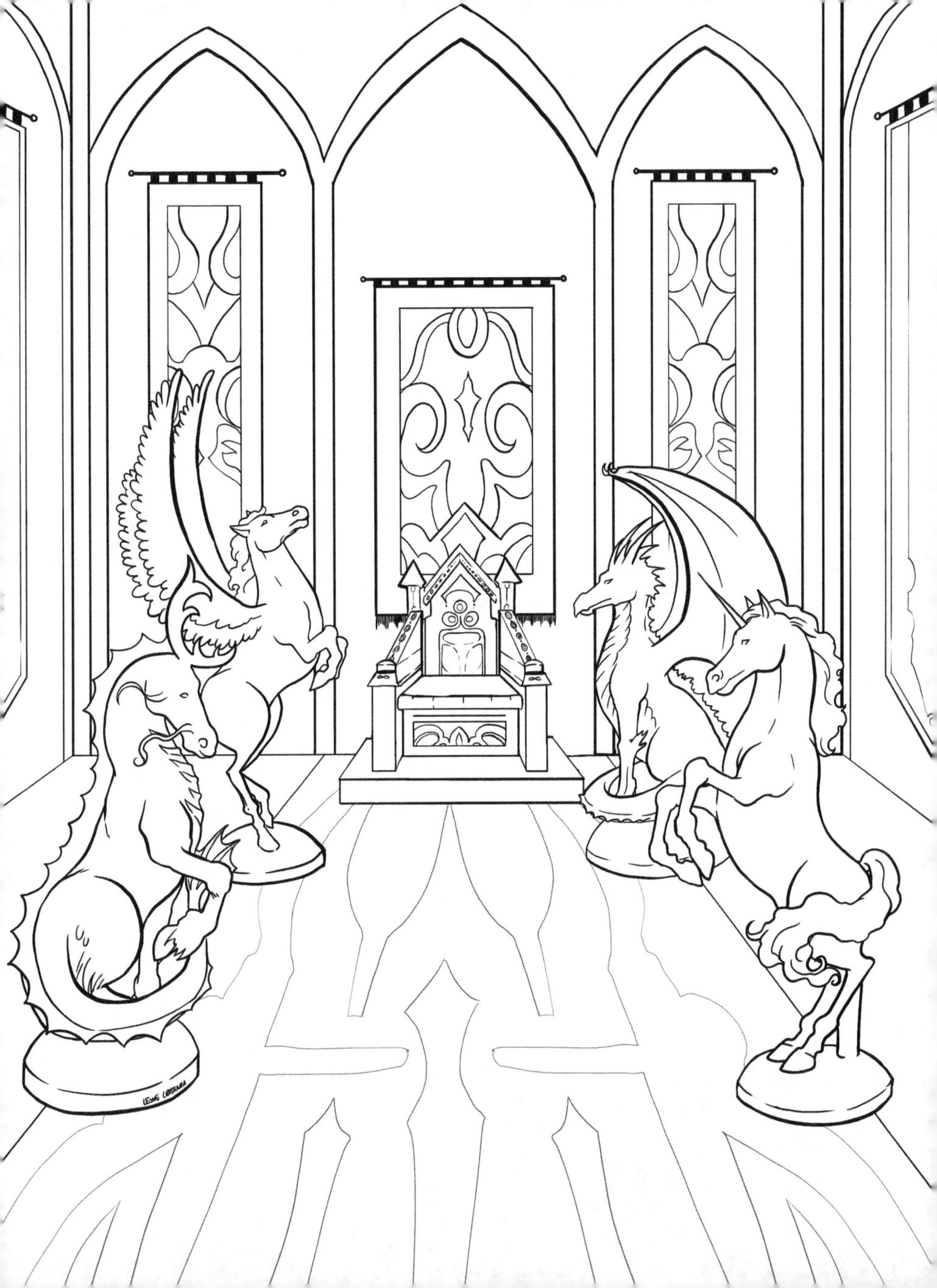

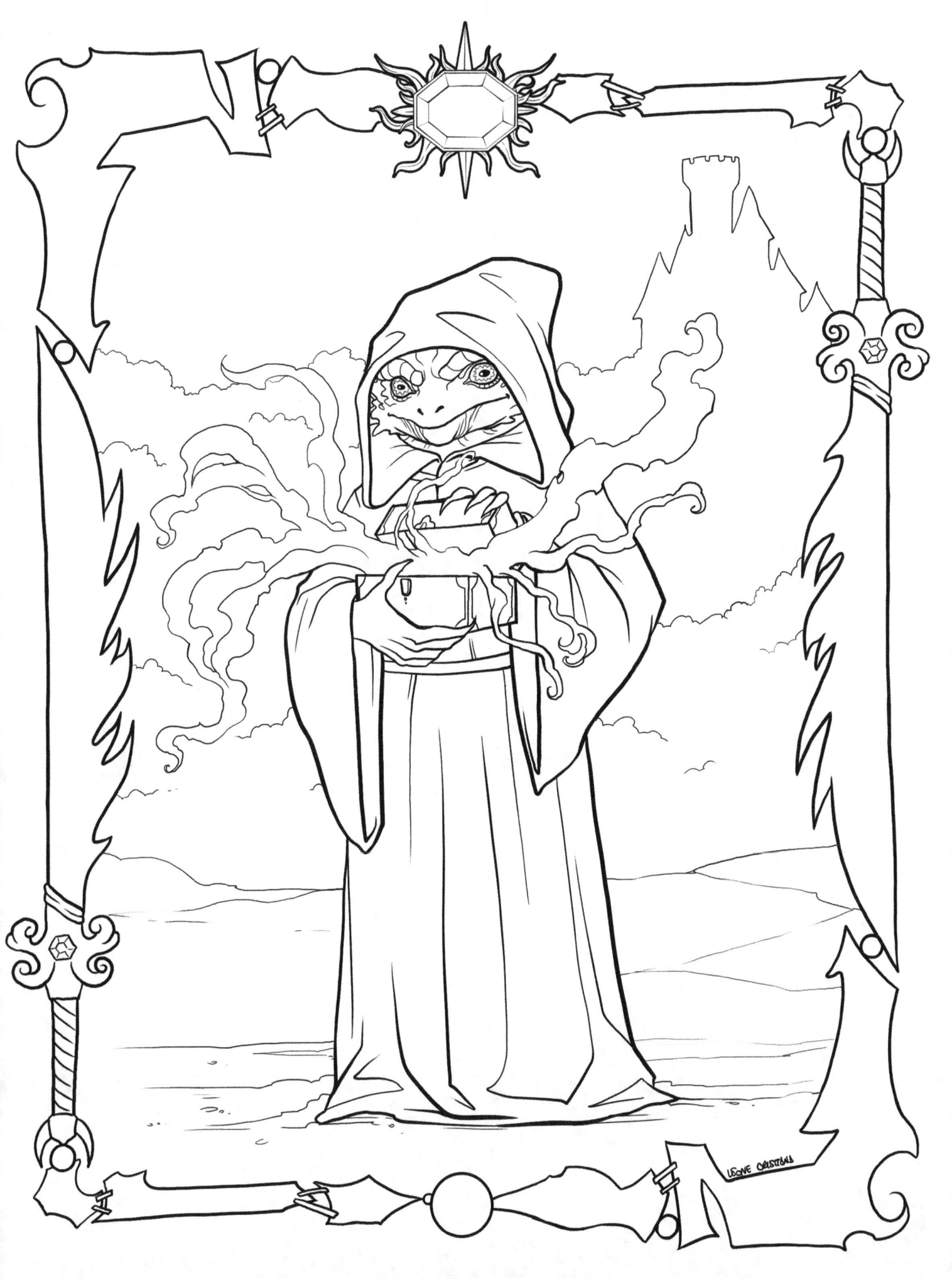

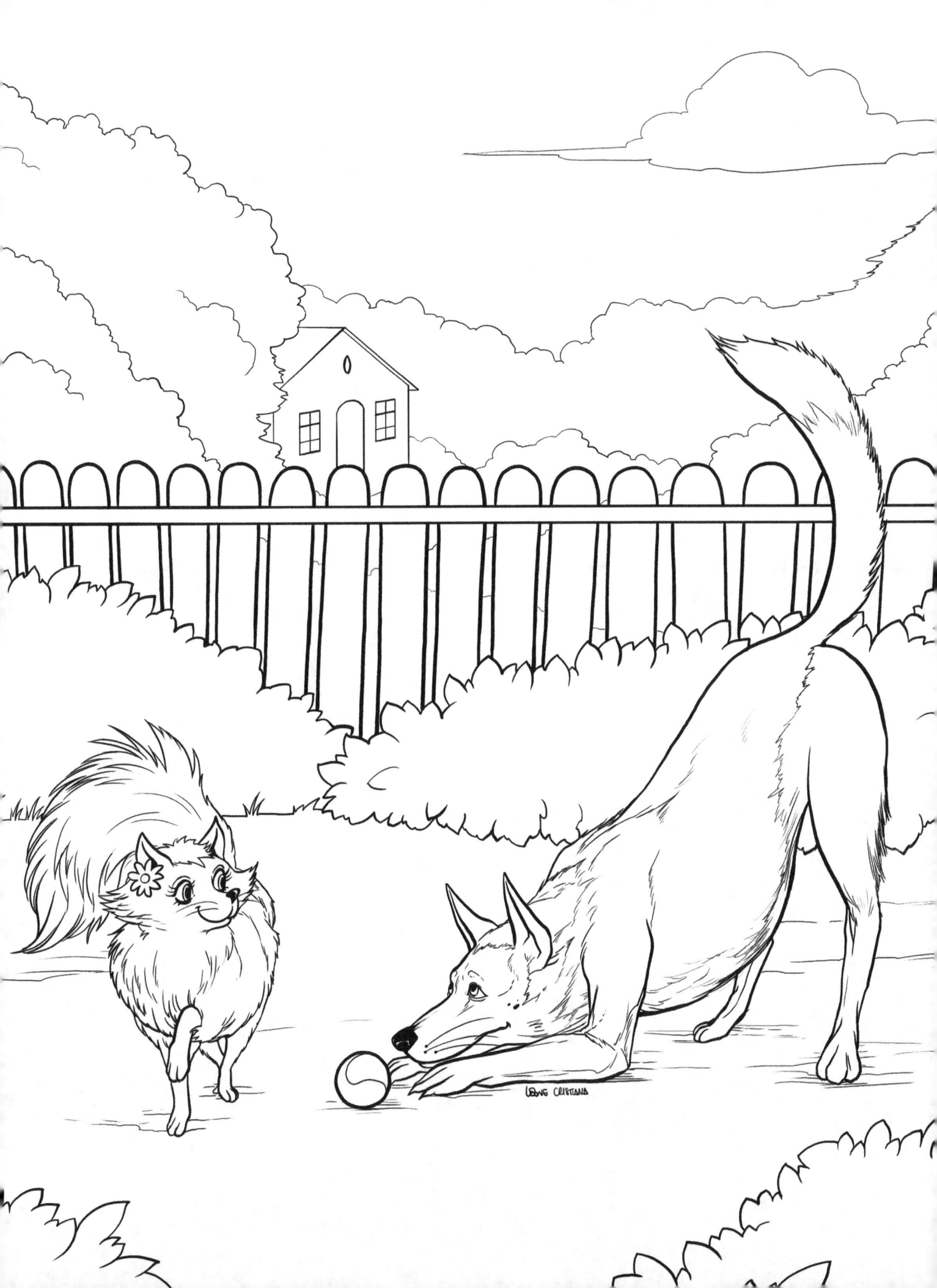

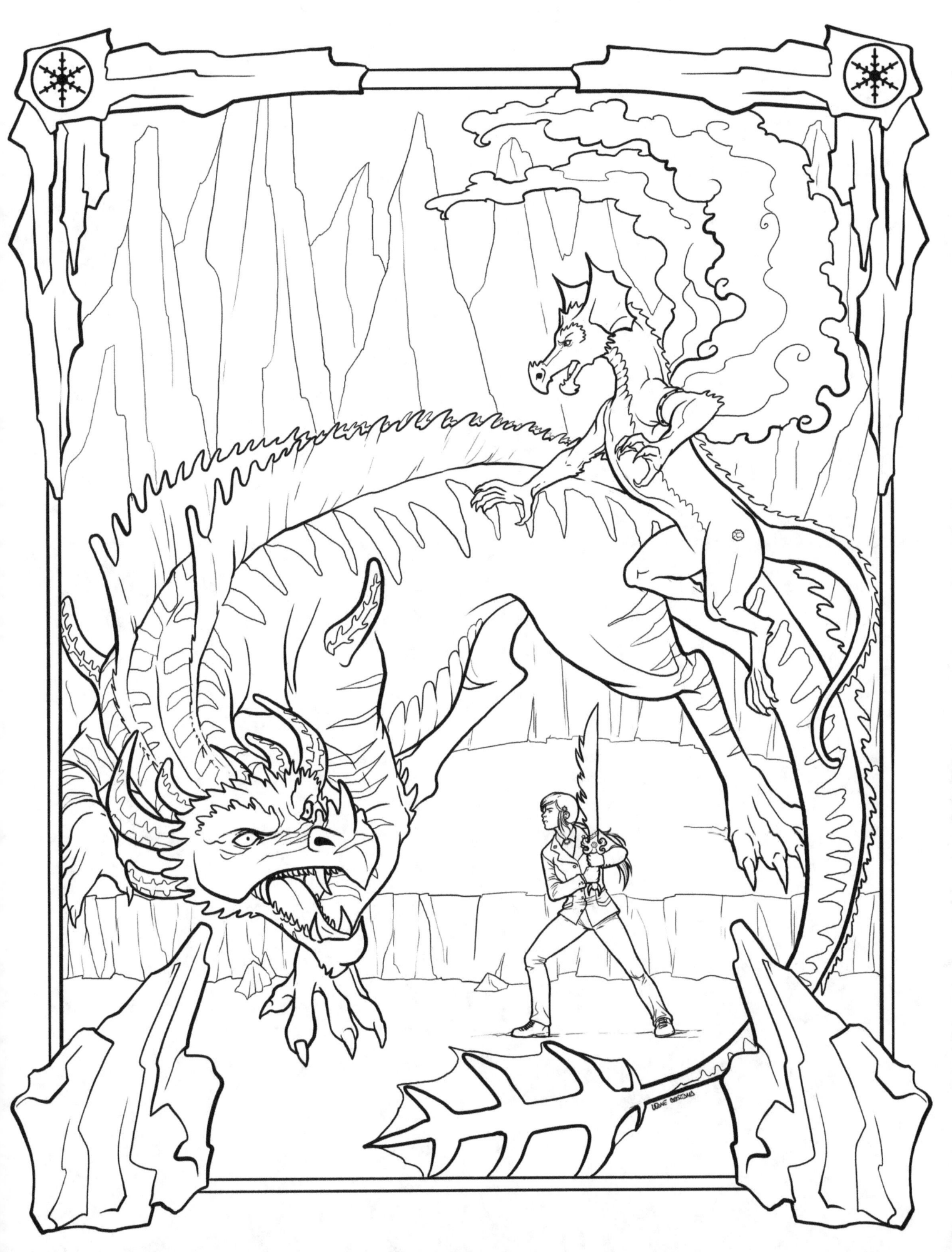

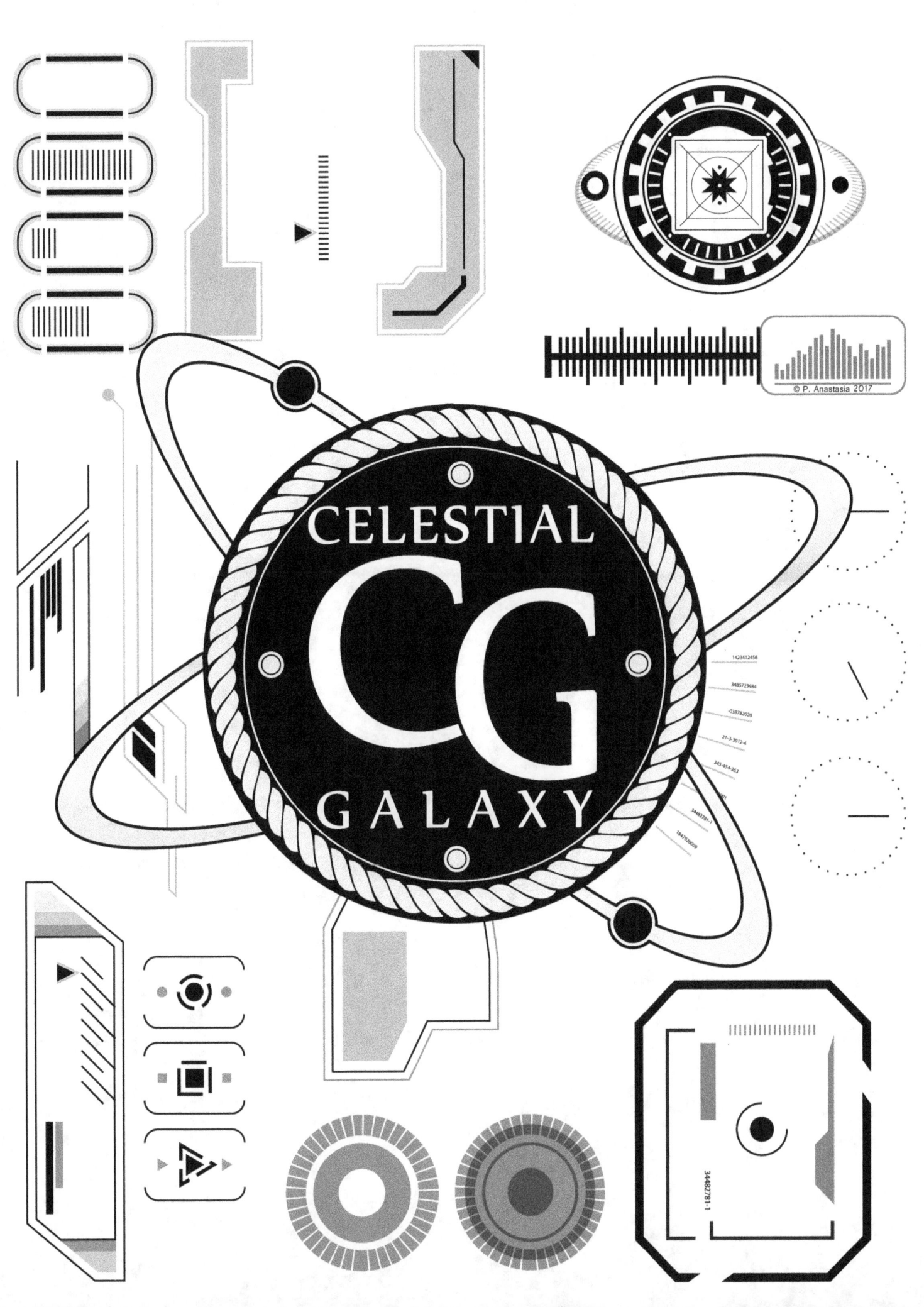

CELESTIAL

CG

GALAXY

© P. Anastasia 2017

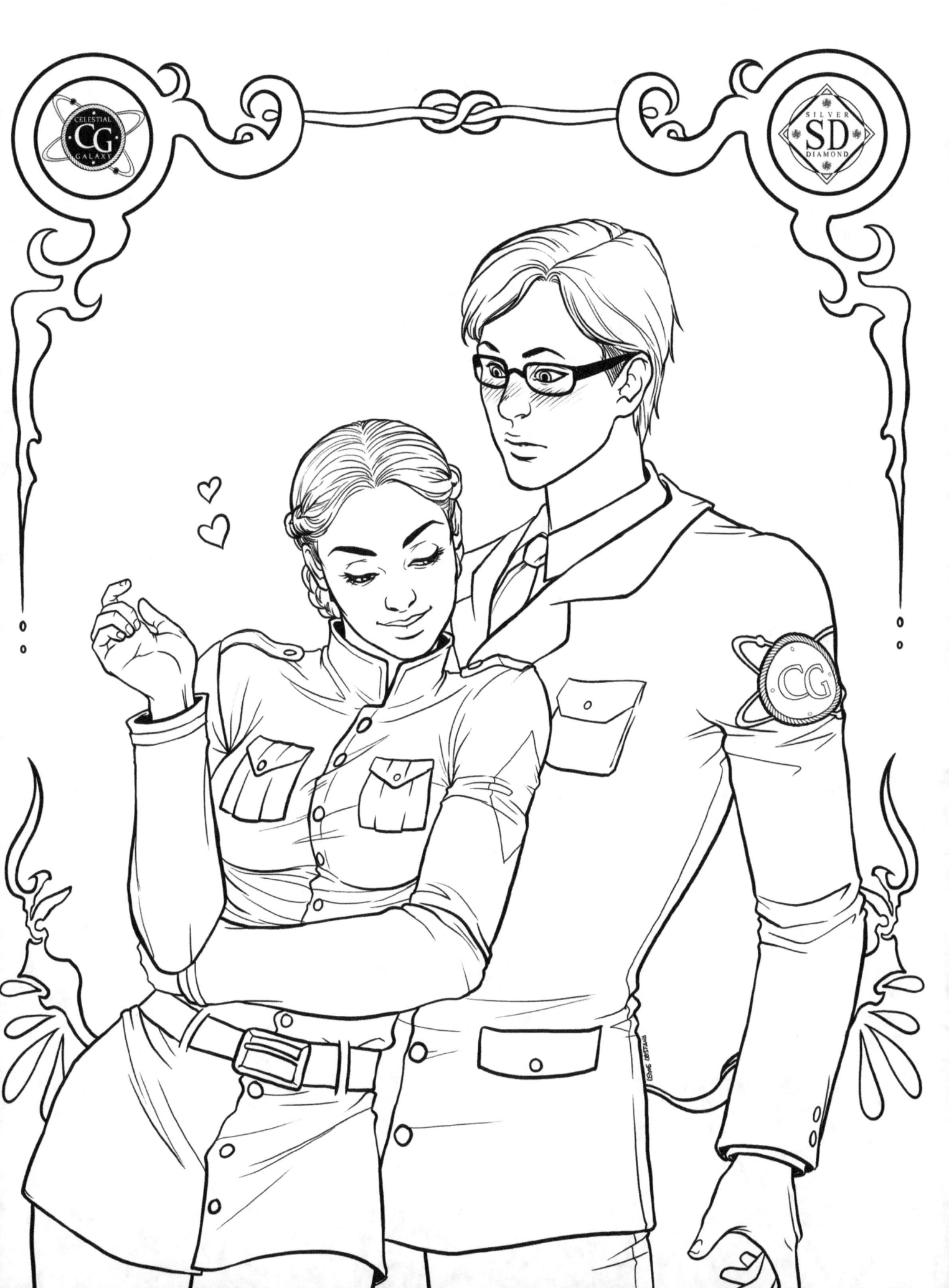

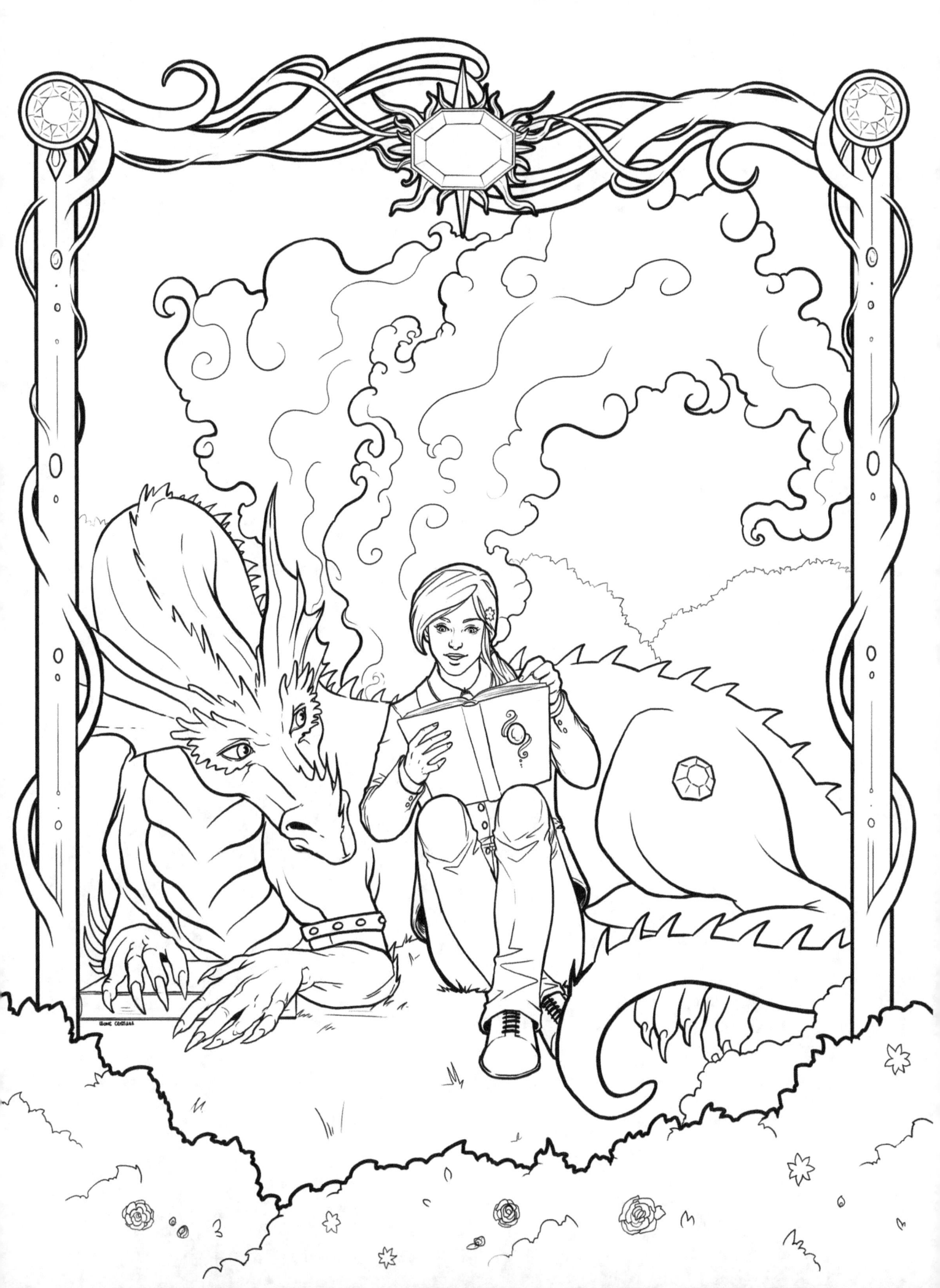

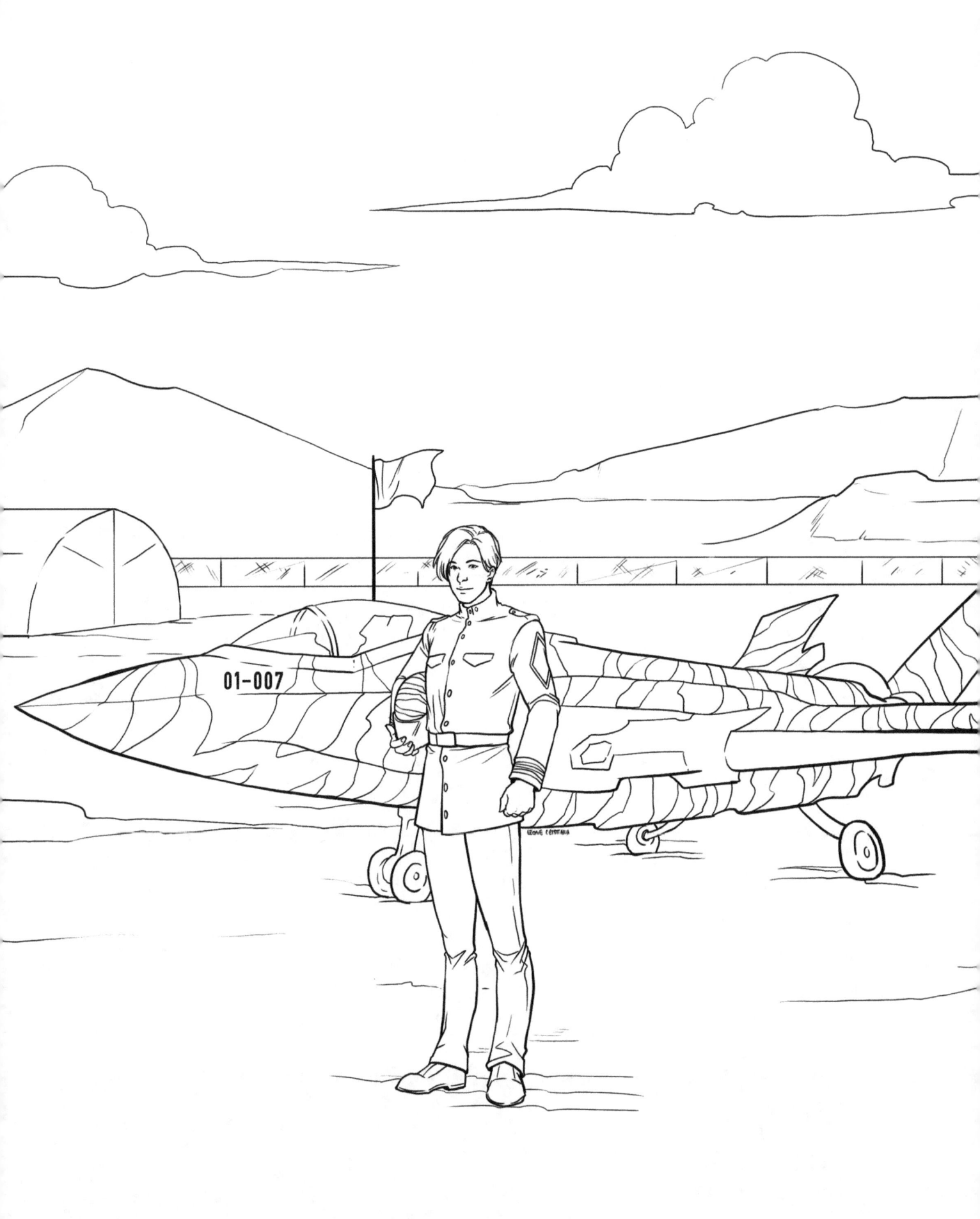

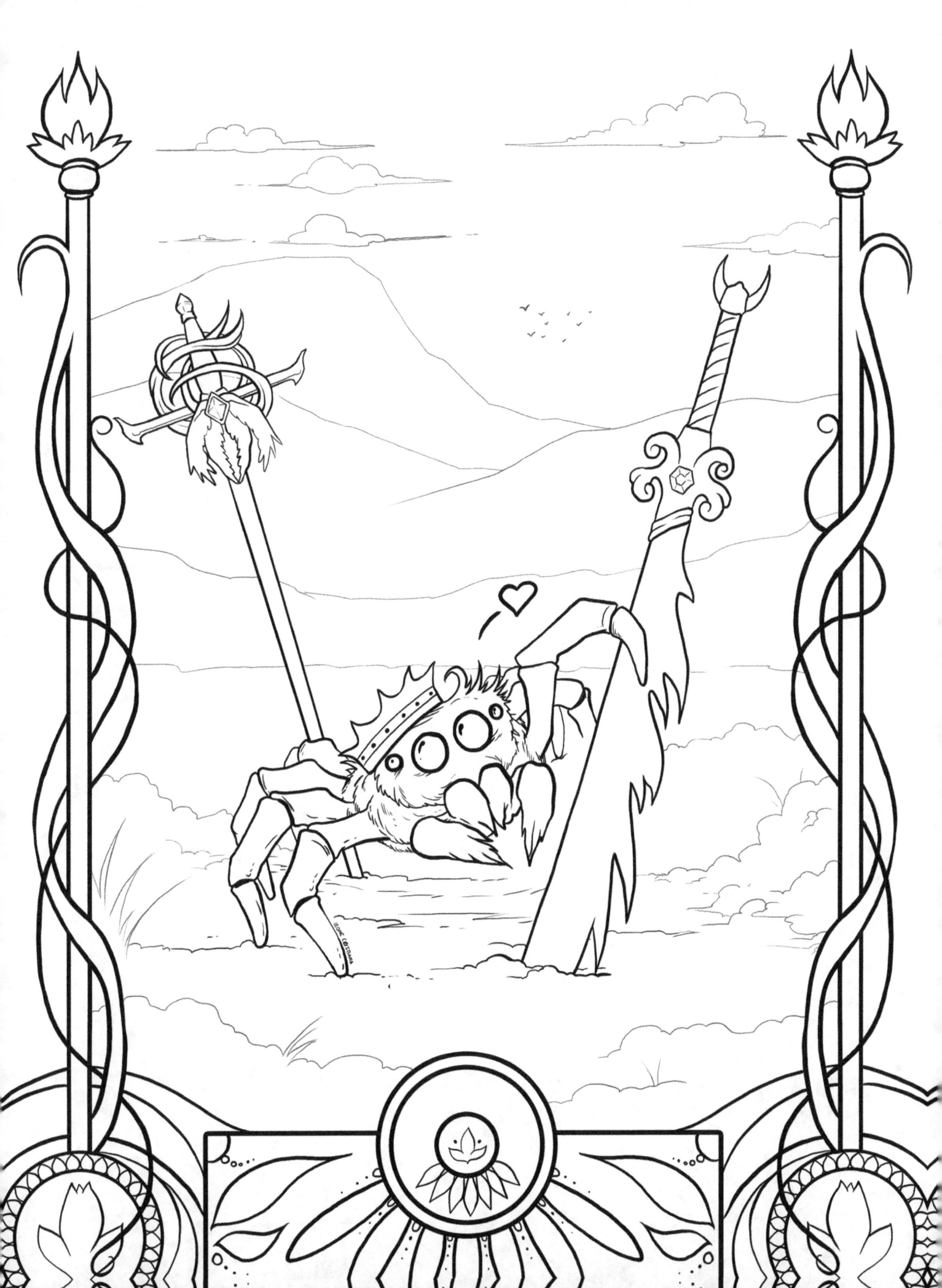

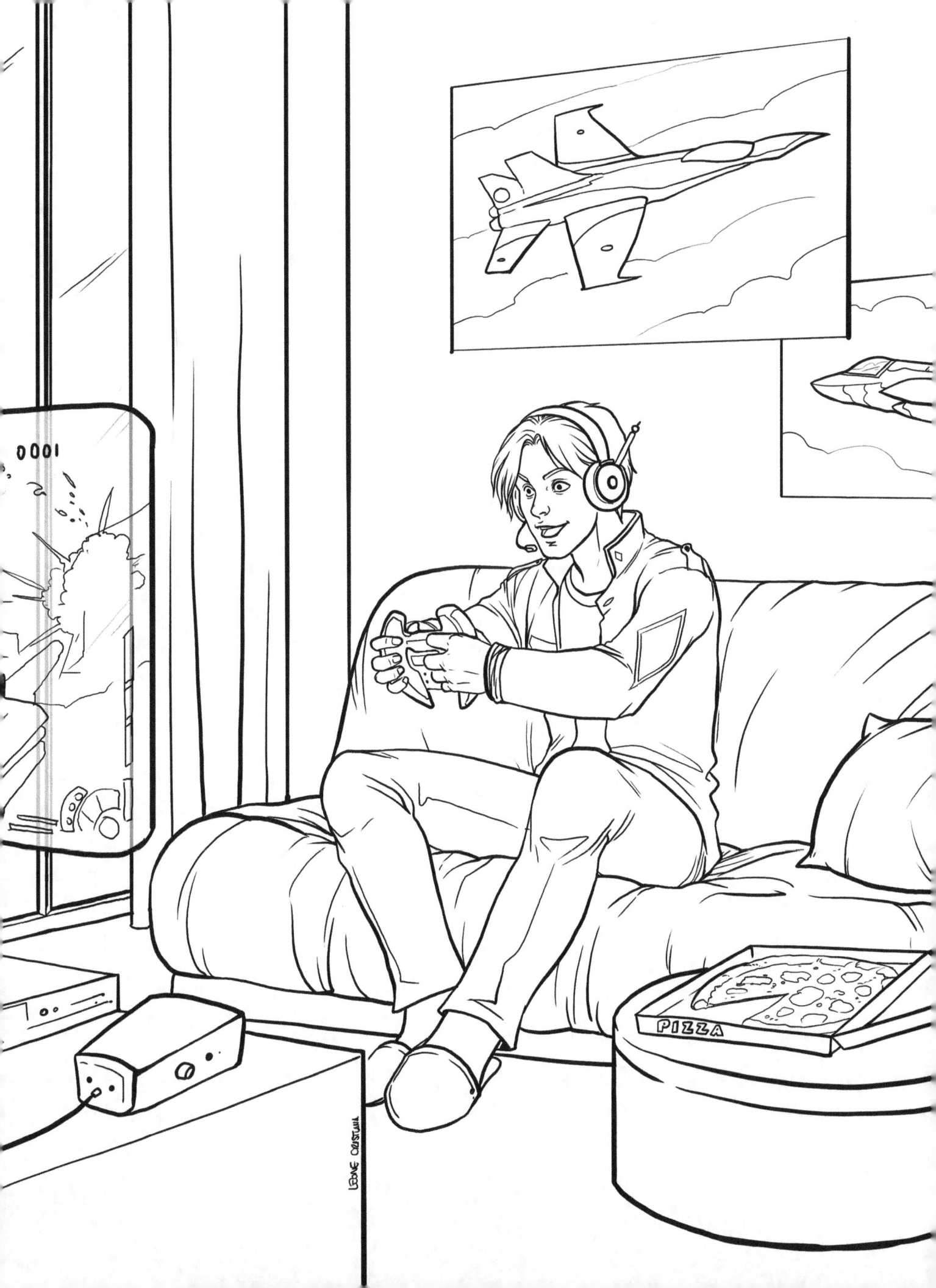

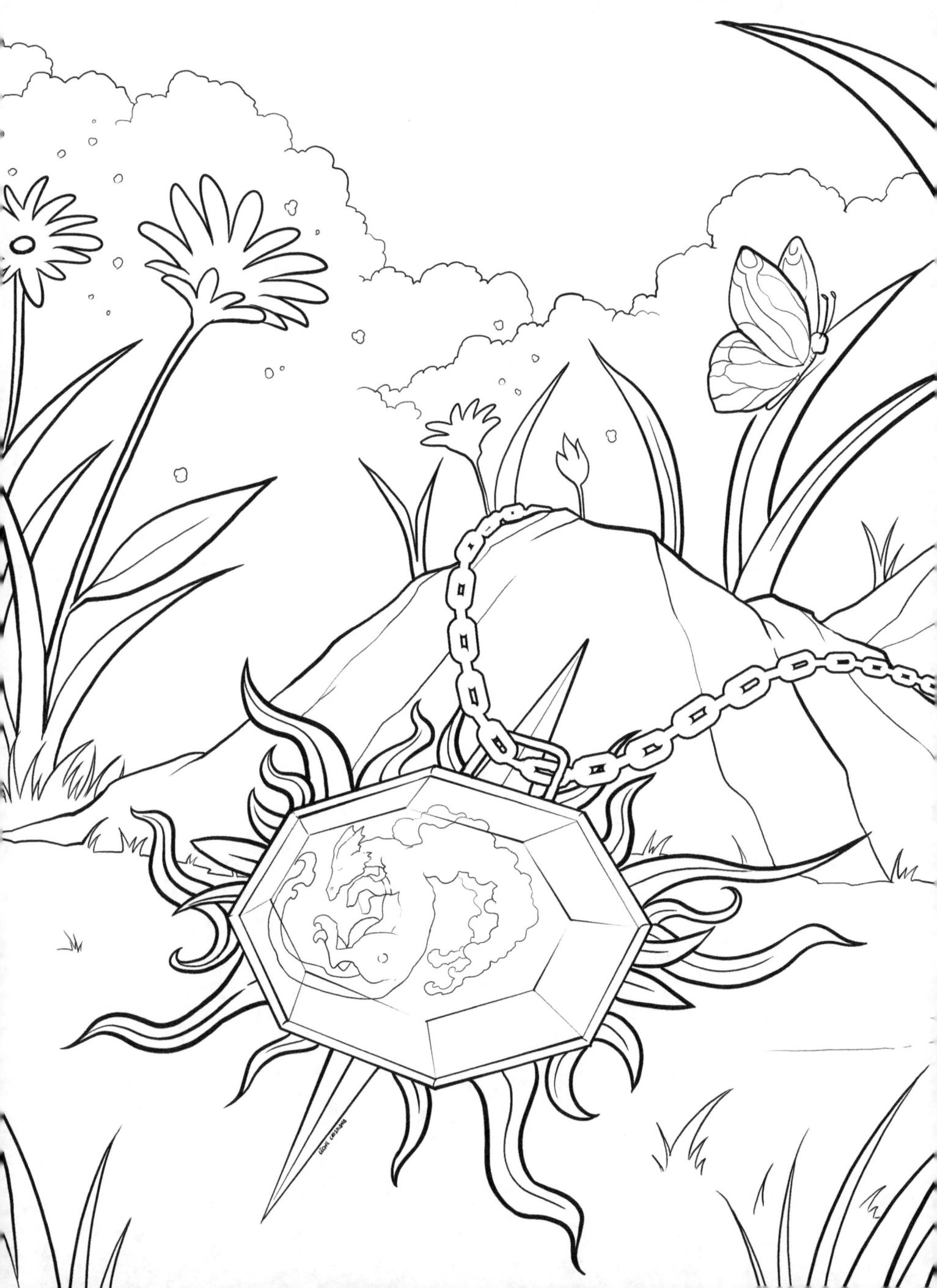

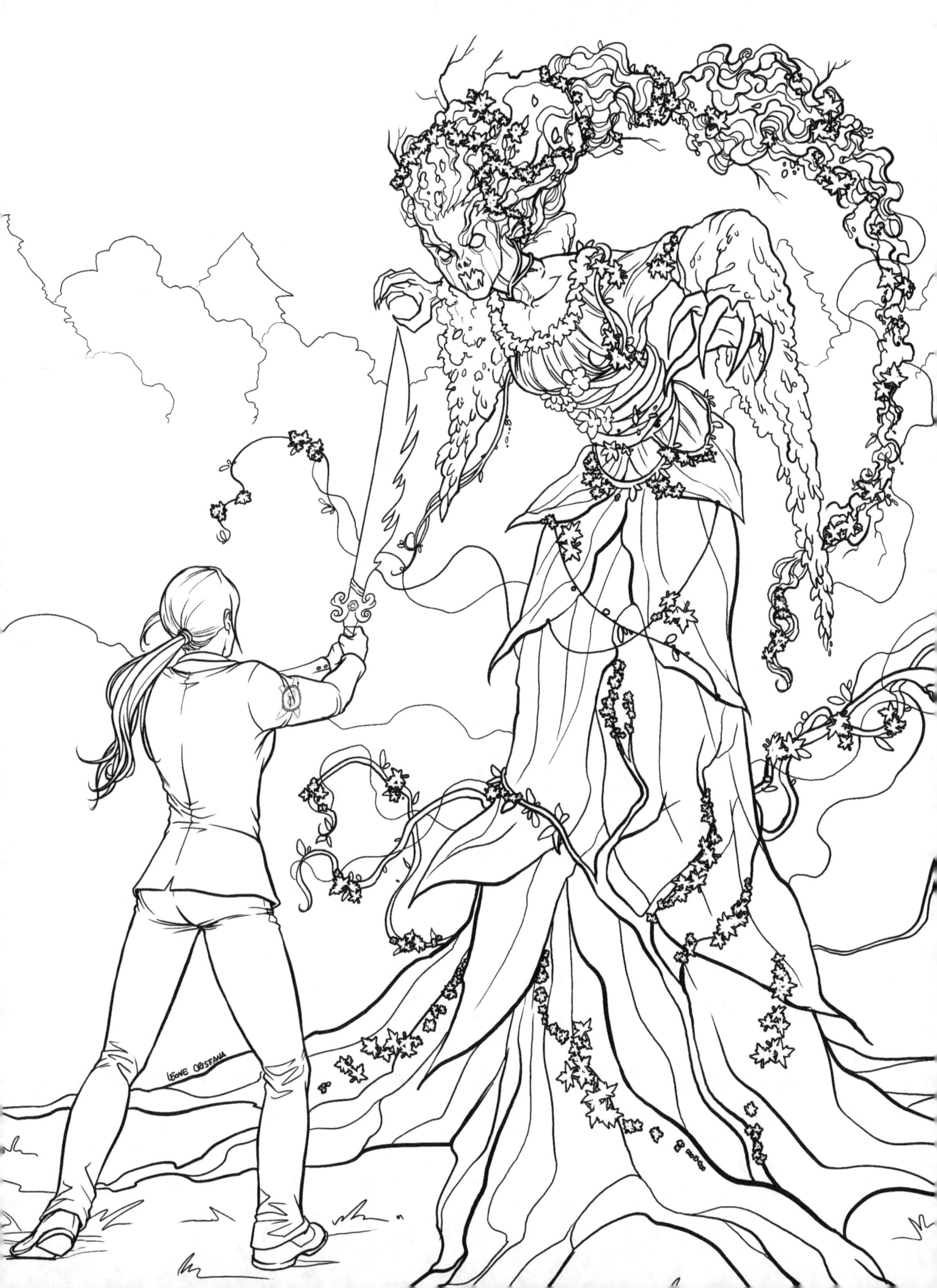

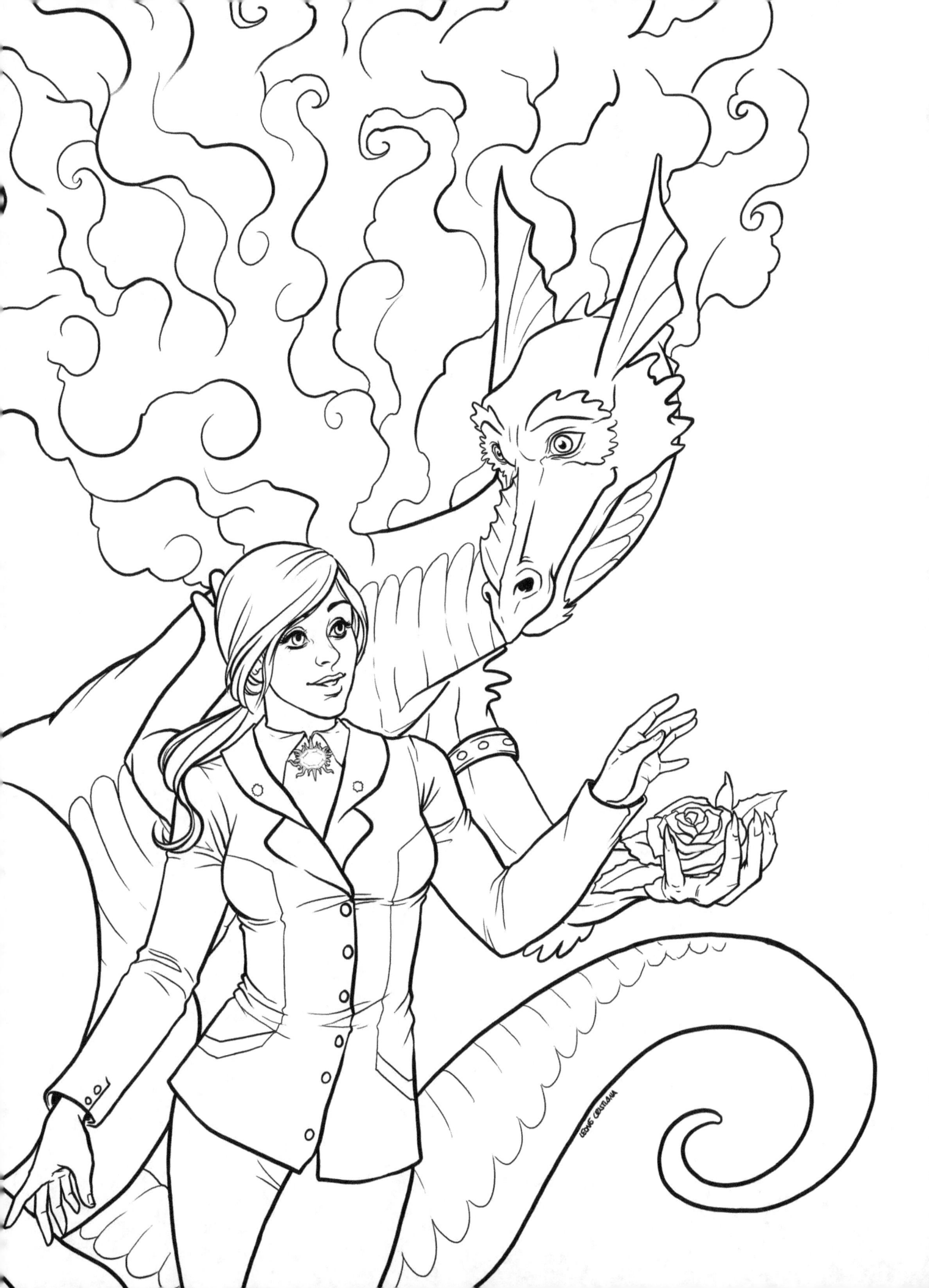

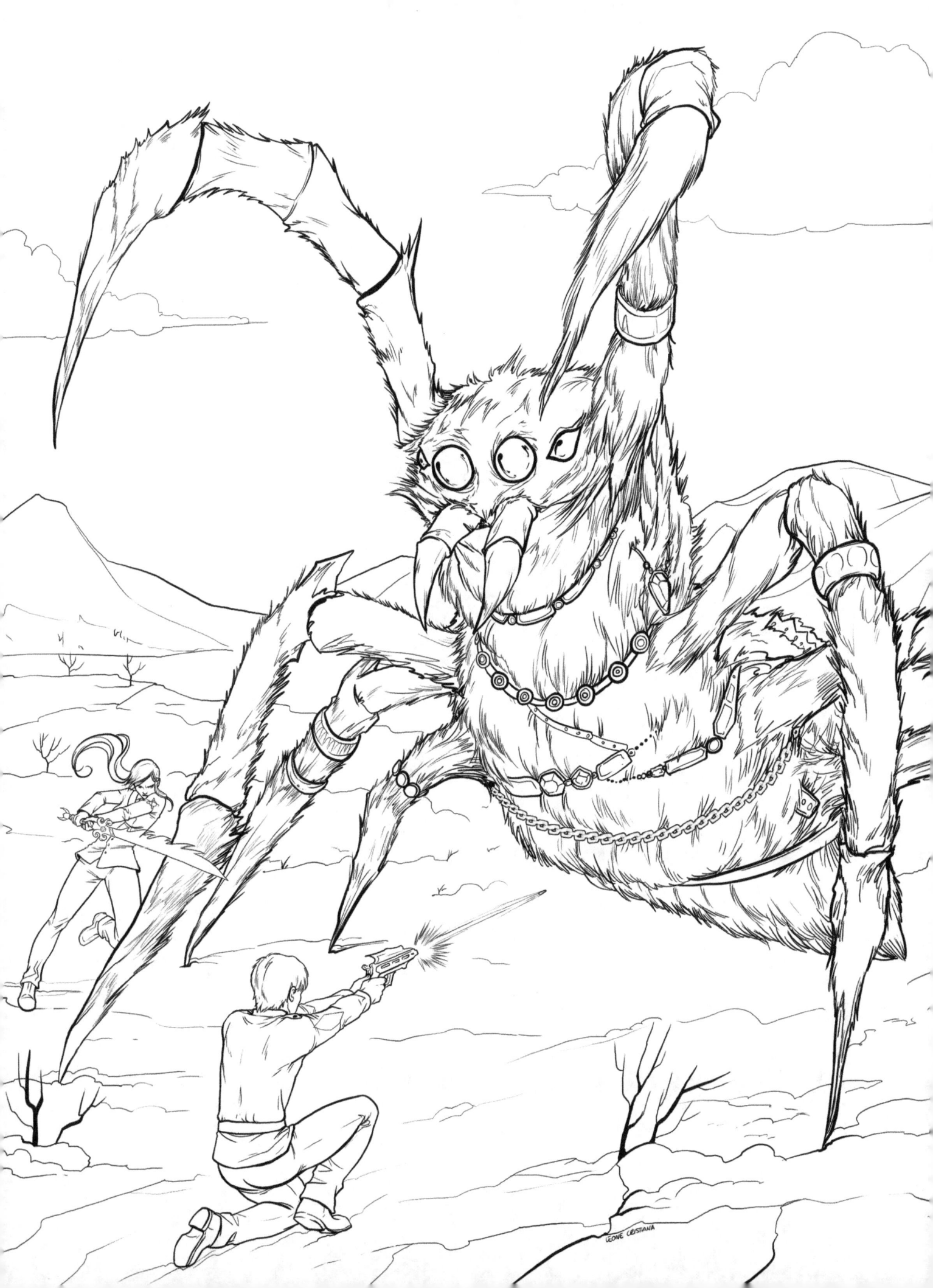

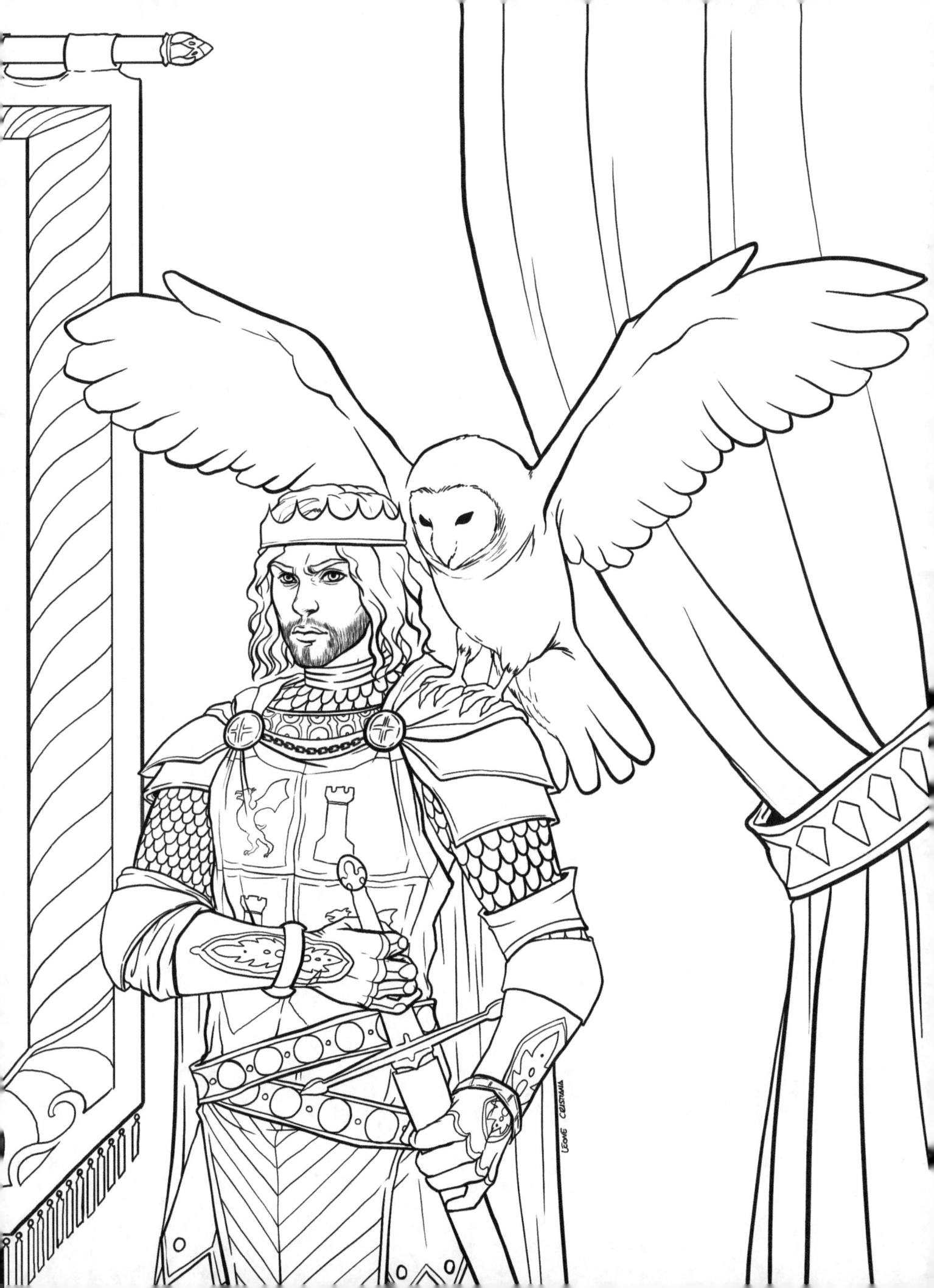

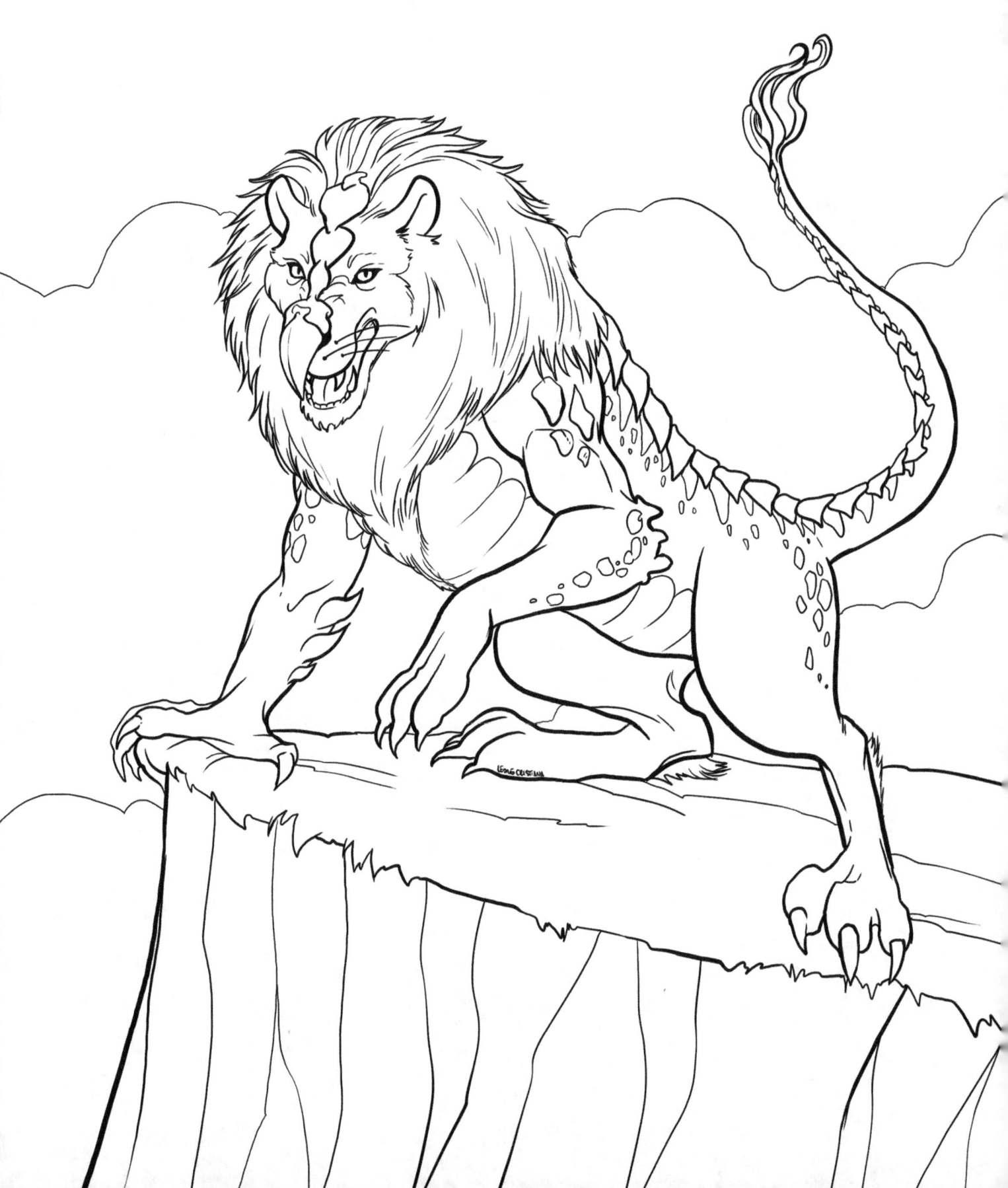

Thank you for purchasing my coloring book!

I hope you enjoyed coloring my world!
Please consider leaving a review on Amazon. It's easy, only
takes a moment, and helps other coloring enthusiasts find and support my works.

For more information on the *Fates Aflame* series, visit FatesAflame.com

Special thanks to my dear friend, Cristiana. Without her, this would not have been possible.
Please visit her site for information on her exciting comic series, *Sunken*.

Stay Radiant!

~P.

ENJOY YOUR FREE BONUS COLORING PAGE!

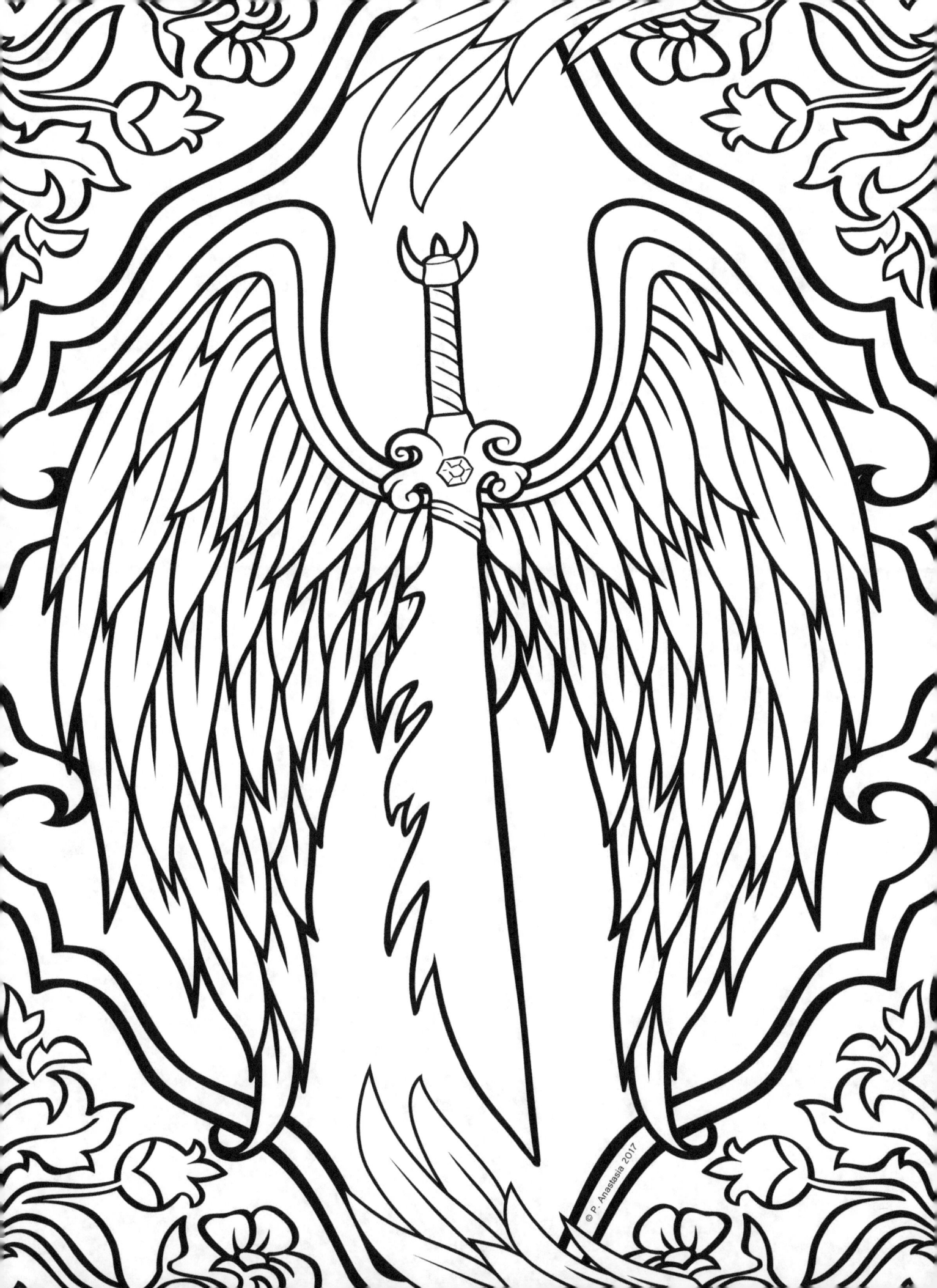